MENNONITE COLONIZATION IN MEXICO

An Introduction

By

J. WINFIELD FRETZ

Published by
THE MENNONITE CENTRAL COMMITTEE
AKRON, PENNSYLVANIA
1945

CONTENTS

Printed in the U.S.A.

A Typical Mennonite Farm Home in Mexico
Buildings are Made of Adobe Brick

Two Old Colony Mennonite Women in Town at Cuauhtemoc, Chihuahua. (Pronounced kwa-te-moc and chi-wa-wa)

Sommerfelder Mennonite Church in the State of Chihuahua

A Typical Mennonite Village Cheese Factory

Foreword

Mennonite Colonization In Mexico is presented herewith to all who are interested not only in the history of the Mennonites but in their present and future welfare as a Christian brotherhood. The booklet is the fruit of a brief study tour undertaken in June, 1944, by Dr. J. Winfield Fretz at the request of the Mennonite Aid Section of the Mennonite Central Committee.

At the time of the trip there was no intention of publishing anything on the Mennonites in Mexico, since the trip was undertaken primarily to gain practical suggestions regarding Mennonite colonization and to aid a prospective Mennonite colonization movement from the United States into that country. The writer was well aware that the Mennonites of Mexico would not welcome publicity and had fully intended to respect their unspoken wishes. However, the information gathered was so impressive, and the interest of the members of the Mennonite Central Committee in the study was so great, that it was nevertheless decided to proceed with a brief publication. It is hoped that the Mennonites of Mexico will understand and appreciate the interest which their Mennonite neighbors in the United States and Canada have in their experience and will not object to the publication.

The booklet is by no means either a scholarly or an exhaustive study of the Mennonites in Mexico. An authoritative account would have required much more time in the original study tour than was possible, as well as more careful historical, statistical, and interpretative analysis with documentation. The author has not intended to give more than an introduction to the subject, but this introduction is of great interest and contains much of value to those interested in future colonization either in Mexico or elsewhere. For this reason it is being published as a second booklet in the series of publications issued by the Mennonite Aid Section of the Mennonite Central Committee. The title, *Mennonite Colonization in Mexico*, indicates the focal point of the study, for in this booklet the Mennonites in Mexico are viewed primarily as colonies rather than as churches. The interest is specifically on the techniques of colonization, and the forms of social and economic organization, and the outcomes in culture as well as in successful community building and economic prosperity. This does not mean that the religious aspects are of minor significance (in fact they are central) but rather that doctrinal and spiritual aspects of Mennonite life in Mexico were not comprehensively treated.

The author is concerned about the future of the Mennonites in Mexico, and rightly so. Nevertheless it is not the purpose of this booklet to point out or even suggest any course to be followed by those who have already staked so much in the great colonization enterprise in our neighbor country to the south. It may be that mutual concern and mutual aid across the boundary lines of nations and church organizations will find expression as time goes on, if need requires. In any case it is certain that the Mennonites of the United States and Canada will follow with much interest and sympathy the future progress of the Mennonite colonies in Mexico.

Harold S. Bender,
For the Mennonite Central Committee.

Mexico in Brief

POPULATION—20,000,000.

LAND AREA—758,258 square miles.

RELIGION—99% Roman Catholic.

LANGUAGE—Spanish.

THE PEOPLE—30% pure Indian; 15% pure White; 55% Mestizo (mixed).

GOVERNMENT—A federal republic composed of twenty-eight states each with an elected governor; a federal president elected every four years.

THE CLIMATE—The country has great diversity of climate, due to its location in both temperate and tropical zones, and due to its varying altitudes. The average annual temperature in the warm lowlands varies from eighty to ninety degrees Fahrenheit, while the plateau temperatures at an altitude of 6,000 feet range from seventy to eighty degrees. Rainfall ranges from 3.0 inches in northern lower California to 81.9 inches in the tropics.

PHYSICAL CHARACTERISTICS — The Sierra Madre Mountain ranges, shaped like a huge wishbone with the two forks reaching north from Mexico City, are the chief markers on the physical map of Mexico. Between the ranges lie a number of valleys and plateaus of differing altitudes.

TRANSPORTATION—The publicly owned National Railways of Mexico cover the country with a network of freight and passenger lines. Connections with American railroads are made at El Paso and Laredo, Texas. Privately owned bus lines serve interior points. The new motor highway from Laredo to Mexico City was opened in 1936 and carries a heavy tourist traffic.

AGRICULTURE—Owing to the rough topography of the land and the climate of the country, large areas of Mexico are unproductive. In 1930 it was estimated that the land of Mexico was utilized as follows: 3.6 percent under cultivation; 3.8 percent fallow crop land; 33.8 pasture; 13.2 forest; 45.6 all other. With a moderate expenditure of money it has been computed that the total crop land could be increased to 11.9 percent by means of irrigation systems.

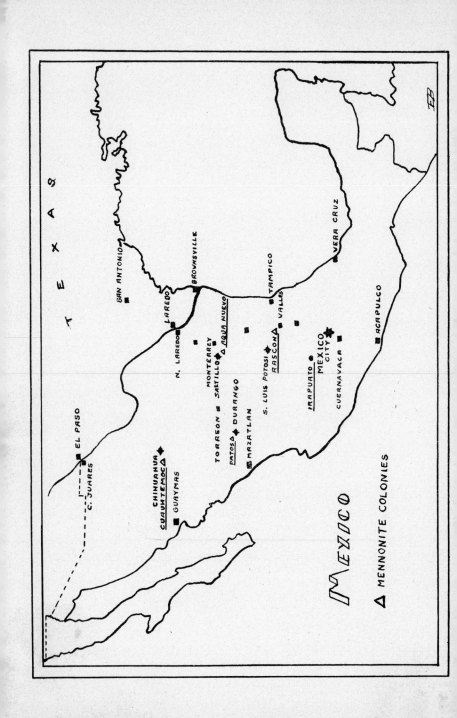

I

Who are the Mennonites of Mexico?

It is a source of surprise to Mennonites in the United States to discover that Mexico is the home of over 12,000 Mennonites. To date Mennonites in the States have known very little about their brethren across the Southern Border and most Mennonites in Mexico have known little about their brethren in the United States. There are probably good historical reasons to account for this situation. The following brief sketch should in part eliminate this condition as far as the Mennonites in the United States are concerned.

OLD COLONY MENNONITES

Of the total number of Mennonites in Mexico, 11,698 belong to the group known as the Old Colony Mennonites. These are to the Mennonites from Russia what the Old Order Amish are to the Mennonites coming from Switzerland, the most conservative group in both cases.

The Old Colony Mennonites or "Altkolonier Reinlaender Mennoniten Gemeinde," as they are called in German, have a long and interesting history. The name "Old Colony" is descriptive of an actual historical situation going back to Russia. It refers to the first settlement of Mennonites on the Crown lands of South Russia in 1789 in the region of Chortitz. In 1803 a second settlement was made on the Molotschna river and this was called the Molotschna colony. During the nineteenth century a large number of new Mennonite settlements were established in Russia, but the first settlement at Chortitz was always referred to as the "Old Colony." The Mennonites who migrated from the Chortitz to Manitoba in 1874-1880 and from there to Mexico in the third decade of the twentieth, continued to be referred to as Old Colony Mennonites wherever they went.

The name is fitting in a sociological as well as a historical sense because throughout the last century and a half this group of Mennonites has made persistent effort to retain all of the old customs, practices and beliefs of their forefathers. Wherever they migrated they tried to reproduce and preserve as accurately as possible the whole social and economic system that they and their forefathers had in former times. Their settlement in villages, their pattern of building arrangements, their mode of dress, their attitudes of non-conformity to the world, their church and community organization, their system of land holding, their attitude toward education and the use of the German language were always transmitted from generation to generation and from colony to colony with as little change as possible.

The story of the mass migration of 5,000 Old Colony Mennonites into Mexico is one of the unwritten chapters of Mennonite History. This group of Mennonites demonstrated all the stout courage, persistence, industriousness, and amazing resourcefulness exhibited by any previous pioneering groups. The Mennonites in Mexico represent a significant block in the agricultural population of Mexico not because of their numerical strength but because of the type of agriculture introduced and the effect upon native methods. Mexico as a country has attracted few European settlers and still fewer religious agricultural groups, such as the Mennonites. Our purpose here is not to give the history of the Old Colony Mennonites but merely to identify them and in the succeeding pages give brief glimpses into the life and customs of the group.

Sommerfelder Mennonites

In addition to the Old Colony Mennonites, there are approximately 600 Sommerfelder Mennonites in Mexico. This group split from the Old Colony in Canada in the 1890's because of the desire for a more progressive school system, and came to Mexico approximately the same time as the Old Colony. The larger portion of the Sommerfelder Mennonites migrated to Paraguay rather than to Mexico.

Church of God in Christ, Mennonite

A third group is the Church of God in Christ, Mennonite, sometimes better known as the Holdeman Mennonites. This small group has a membership of about sixty-five in Mexico. The Holdeman Mennonites came to Mexico in 1927 as a small group of five families from Isabella, Oklahoma. They have added to their original group five families of converted native Mexicans. They are the only Mennonite group to carry on active mission work among the Mexicans. The group is at present located at the northern end of the Old Colony settlement in Chihuahua, but is planning to move to Paradise Valley near Saltillo, eight hundred miles southeast of their present location. They have bought a 12,500-acre tract of land for this purpose.

GENERAL CONFERENCE MENNONITES

A fourth branch of the Mennonites is the General Conference Mennonite group consisting of one congregation of about fifty souls in the City of Cuauhtemoc in the State of Chihuahua. This group is composed of Mennonites who came directly from Russia as refugees in the twenties. There were formerly about fifty additional Mennonite refugee families from Russia in Mexico who could not enter the United States or Canada directly chiefly for health reasons. After several years in Mexico all but about a dozen families succeeded in getting to Canada or the United States.

OLD ORDER MENNONITES AND OLD ORDER AMISH

The fifth group of Mennonites in Mexico is also the most recent. It consists of four Old Order Mennonite and two Old Order Amish families, located in the State of San Luis Potosi, and comprises a total of thirty-six souls. This latter group came to Mexico during the early spring of 1944, most of them from Lancaster County, Pennsylvania. None of the families have yet bought land, and the settlement to date is by no means permanent.

In this following brief sketch of the Mennonites in Mexico, major attention will be paid to the Old Colony Mennonites because of their preponderance in numbers, their significance for the life of Mexico, and their interest to the Mennonites in the United States.

II
Why did the Mennonites go to Mexico?

All of the Old Colony and Sommerfelder Mennonites migrated to Mexico from Canada between 1922 and 1927. They left Canada because the educational privileges granted them in 1874 were taken away from them. Following World War I the Canadian Government attempted to nationalize all of its ethnic groups except the French. One of its methods was to insist that schools be conducted in the English language, although German could still be taught as one of the subjects. Previously ethnic groups were allowed to conduct their own schools pretty much as they pleased. When the new decree was issued, denying the original privileges granted the Mennonites, the Old Colony Mennonites decided to migrate rather than surrender freedom of education. To surrender complete freedom of education was to them the equivalent of surrendering freedom of religion.

FINDING A NEW HOME

A delegation of six men first investigated colonization possibilities in a number of South American countries but chiefly in Argentina, Brazil and Uraguay. The delegation was unable to secure the desired privileges in any of these countries. By sheer accident the Mennonites chanced to engage in conversation with the Mexican Consul in Buenos Aires as they were waiting on the pier to return to Canada. After hearing their story the Consul invited the delegation to visit Mexico and promised them all the freedoms for their people they were looking for. In addition, he assured them that economic and political conditions in Mexico were more favorable than they had previously thought. After the delegation reached Canada and reported its failure to find a land of freedom in South America, it was immediately dispatched on a similar scouting trip to Mexico. After several journeys to Mexico City and at least five meetings with President Alvaro Obregon, the desired privileges were granted. These privileges are in the form of a presidential decree rather than an act of law provided by the Mexican Congress. This accounts for the informal and personal nature of the charter of special privileges. The concessions granted the Mennonites are given in the following translated* letter from President Obregon:

SPECIAL PRIVILEGES

"To the representatives of the Old Colony Reinland Mennonite Church, Rev. Julius Loewen, Johann Loeppky, Director Benjamin Goertzen and members Cornelius Rempel, Klaas Heide and David Rempel.

"In reply to your letter of January 29, 1921, in which you express the desire to establish yourselves in this country as agricultural settlers, I have the honor of giving you the following information in answer to the specific questions contained in the letter referred to above.

1.   You will not be forced to accept military service.

2.   In no case will you be compelled to swear oaths.

3.   You will be completely free to exercise your religious principles and to observe the regulations of your church without being molested or restricted in any way.

4.   You are fully authorized to establish your own schools, with your own teachers, without any hindrance from the Government.   Concerning this point our laws are exceedingly liberal.

5.   You may dispose of your property in any way you may desire.   This Government will raise no objections to the establishment among the members of your sect of any economic system which they may voluntarily want to adopt.

"It is the most ardent desire of this Government to provide favorable conditions to colonists such as Mennonites who love order, lead moral lives, and are industrious. Therefore we would deem it a pleasure if this answer would satisfy you.   The aforementioned privileges being guaranteed by our laws, we hope, that you will take advantage of them positively and permanently.

(Sufragio efectivo No Reeleccion)

Mexico, February 25, 1921

The constitutional President of the United States of Mexico

A. Obregon

Secretary of Agriculture and Economic Affairs

A. I. Villareal

"In reply to your request of October 27, presented by your representatives Arturo J. Braniff and Johann E. Wiebe, I have the honor to inform you that you can at any time rely upon legal protection for your life and property.

"Furthermore I want to assure you that you are allowed to conduct both school and church in the German language.

Sufragio efectivo No Reeleccion.
Mexico, D. F. October 30, 1921
Sign. A. Obregon
Sign. J. Villareal
Secretary of Agriculture and Economic Affairs."*

Immediately after receiving the above assurance the Old Colony Mennonites made plans to dispose of real estate in Canada, and as rapidly as possible moved to Mexico. In the beginning, from seventy-five to ninety-five percent of the Old Colony group was in favor of migration. However, before all the land was sold enthusiasm for migration began to decline. Discouraging reports from the first settlers had come back, propaganda within the colony by those opposed to moving had taken effect, and prosperous economic conditions of the colonies at home, in contrast to the uncertainty and prospective struggle of settlement in a foreign land, resulted in a large number deciding not to migrate. It is reported that less than fifty percent of the Old Colony people in Canada actually moved to Mexico. Some of those migrating became discouraged and later returned to Canada.

*Translated from the Spanish by Beatrice Buller.

III

Where did the Mennonites Settle in Mexico?

The Mennonites settled in the northern semi-arid regions of Mexico in the State of Chihuahua. Here 10,000 Mennonites are settled. They are located in what is known as the San Antonio Valley which is surrounded by low lying mountains and hills. The elevation in this area is between six and seven thousand feet above sea level. As a consequence, the winter season is somewhat long with cool weather and frosts to be expected as early as October and extending into the months of April and May. Snowfall in the region is practically unknown. The average annual rainfall in and about the Chihuahua settlement is reported to be from sixteen to eighteen inches with frequently recurring dry years. Practically all of the land in the area is adapted to dry farming with surface water available at depths up to seventy feet.

The Mennonites in the State of Chihuahua are made up of various groups. The Old Colony Mennonites are settled in two adjacent colonies, one known as the Manitoba Colony, consisting of 7,225 souls; the other known as the Swift Current Colony with 2,122 souls. Both colonies derive their names from their place of origin in Canada. The settlement is located seventy-five miles west of the city of Chihuahua, which is two hundred thirty miles south of El Paso, Texas, and can be reached by a well improved modern highway. In addition to the two Old Colony settlements in Chihuahua there is a small settlement of about six hundred Sommerfelder Mennonites who live to the extreme north end of the Old Colony in what is called the Santa Clara area. A third group, namely the Holdeman Mennonites, consisting of sixty-five souls, are located between the Old Colony and the Sommerfelder group. The fourth group of Mennonites, known as the General Conference people, are located in the City of Cuauhtemoc which is at the southern end of the entire Mennonite settlement. It is a city of about eight thousand people, located seventy-five miles west of the capital city of Chihuahua and is connected with that center by motor highway, bus route, and railroad.

State of Durango

A third Old Colony Mennonite settlement, consisting of 2,151 souls and called the "Hague Colony" is located in the State of Durango about seventy miles northwest of the capital city of Durango. It is the only group of Mennonites in this state. The shopping center and railroad station for the Hague Colony Mennonites is called Patos. The settlement is referred to as the Hague Colony because of its original location near Hague, Sasketchewan. It is of historical interest that originally all of the Old Colony group had planned to settle in the State of Durango. In fact, land had already been bought there by the Manitoba Colony but was later exchanged for land in Chihuahua before settlers actually arrived.

Although the Durango Colony is five hundred miles to the southeast of the Manitoba Colony, the climatic factors and geographic conditions are very similar in both states. In Durango the rainfall is slightly heavier and the climate slightly milder than in Chihuahua.

State of Nuevo Leon

A word should be added about the locations of two new groups which attempted settlement in the early spring of 1944. Thirty-eight families from the Manitoba Colony moved to the State of Nuevo Leon about thirty miles south of the City of Saltillo, approximately five hundred miles southeast of the large settlement in Chihuahua. The area has climatic factors much similar to those in the former location. The elevation, however, is only about five thousand feet and the soil is much more difficult to make productive. Water resources are also seemingly inadequate. At the time of the writer's visit the new settlers were greatly discouraged, and it has since become known that about three-fourths of the settlers returned to Chihuahua, with the remainder very likely soon to follow. This represents a loss of thousands of pesos to the unsuccessful and unhappy settlers plus the end of another short-lived Mennonite colonization effort. At the same time that the Old Colony settlers are giving up their colonization effort, the Holdeman Mennonites have bought land in the same area and are planning to move there. The Holdeman settlement will not include over ten families.

State of San Luis Potosi

A small settlement of six Old Order Mennonite and Old Order Amish families is located in a tropical area about one hundred thirty miles inland from the gulf coastal town of Tampico. Here the rainfall is much higher and vegetation much greater. Tropical insects and diseases are also more prevalent here. The topography is rugged and the elevation varies all the way from two to four thousand feet above sea level. This small group has not yet definitely decided upon a location but after having investigated dry farming possibilities in northern Mexico where most of the Mennonites are located, this group decided not to settle there. Coming mostly from Lancaster County, Pennsylvania, this small band of pioneers wished to settle if possible in an area of greater rainfall and under conditions which were similar to those they left in the United States.

IV
What is the Mennonite Pattern of Settlement?

The land bought in Mexico was secured in a single block. It was surveyed, the roads laid out, the villages located, and the farms divided, all before migration actually took place. The villages in Mexico were generally given names of familiar villages in Canada, which names in turn had been brought from Russia. Such descriptive names as the following are characteristic: Blumenthal, Gnadenfeld, Chortitz, Rosenort, Blumengart, Hochfeld, Reinland, Schoenfeld, Neuhoffnung, Gruenfeld, and Schoenthal. The people who lived together in a particular village in Canada generally moved into one village in Mexico. In this way neighbors in the homeland were also neighbors in the new land. The pattern of village settlement in Mexico is identical with that in Canada and that in Canada identical with that in Russia. Each village consists of from ten to thirty farm homes. About half of the homes in each village are distributed on either side of a large broad street. Each farmstead consists of about five acres. This is used for buildings, orchards, gardens, and corrals. The farmland of each family extends a half mile or mile back of the farmstead. Where farmers have large acreage they must sometimes travel several miles to farm it. The farms range from eighty to three hundred sixty acres in size, but the average is about one hundred sixty acres.

LAND OWNERSHIP

Among the Old Colony Mennonites the land of a single colony is still technically owned by one or two men, usually by the Oberschulz and one other individual. The Oberschulz is an elected official who most nearly compares to our conception of a general manager. He is the business man for the colony. The individual Mennonite farmer, although he may have completely paid for his farm, does not legally have title to his land. His only evidence of ownership is the list of paid entries in the record book maintained by the Oberschulz. In this book is recorded the date of purchase, the amount of land bought, and the time and number of payments made throughout the years. When a man has paid for his farm in full the fact is noted in the account book and the record is closed. The individual farmer merely accepts on faith the fact that he has full ownership to the farm. There are always two record books so that checks can be made in case of errors or questions. Honesty on the part of the Oberschulz is of crucial importance to the economic security of the members of the colony, and it is significant that the several thousand families never seem to have had occasion to question the integrity of their leaders on this matter.

Securing New Land

The Mennonites in Mexico, as do Mennonites in other parts of the world, constantly face the problem of securing new land for their ever growing population. The methods by which they solve this problem, however, differ from the methods used by Mennonites in other countries. The striking difference is the systematic and efficient way in which land is acquired. When there is a growing consciousness in the colony that new land is needed, the Oberschulz and his assistants take the initiative in scouting for, and buying new land, as well as discovering who in the colony wants the land. The procedure is as follows: A list of the names of people wanting new land is drawn up and each man states the amount of money he has available for purchase of the land. If he does not have sufficient funds of his own he is urged to borrow the money from a friend or relative. If possible, the total acreage purchased by the colony is always larger than the immediate demand so that there is room for expansion. Money not available for purchase from those who want the land is generally supplied by the men with means in the colony on a loan basis. The creditors receive three or four percent interest and the borrowers pay six percent, the difference being used for administrative purposes.

The interested group of settlers meet with the Oberschulz to draw up a plan of division for the new settlement. Each plot or separate farm is given a number. When the total plan is worked out, the interested parties draw for the number of the farm they are to buy. After the selection, if two individuals wish to exchange their plots they may do so, but they cannot refuse their farm outright in favor of another drawing. Each farm is evaluated in advance according to the quality of the land and its location. Hence the several farms vary in price.

Each new village then organizes by electing its own Schulz, or head man, as well as other public officials in the village. The settlers then select the name for the new village. This is usually a favorite name found among the Mennonite villages in Canada or in Russia. The selecting of new plots of land and their settlement is at present a concern of the growing Old Colony. This systematic method of solving such a basic problem makes the Mennonite policy of land settlement in Mexico significant for Christian rural groups elsewhere.

V

How do the Mennonites Earn Their Living

The first ten years of life in Mexico were exceedingly difficult for the Mennonites. There was the unfamiliar climate, the strange soil, the new weather conditions, the lack of markets for the crops that were produced, the repeated crop failures due to lack of knowledge about local agriculture conditions, and the generally primitive conditions of living in the area in which they settled. In addition to these natural factors, the Mennonites suffered heavy financial losses through bank failures. It was estimated that during the early years of settlement close to one-half million dollars were lost by the Old Colony Mennonites in Chihuahua due to the failure of unstable banks. It was only through persistence and hard work that they were able to overcome these severe setbacks and gradually improve their economic condition so as to be able to continue. However, never during these trying years did they seek or secure relief from outside agencies. They quietly bore their losses, endured hardships and privations, and assisted each other.

AGRICULTURE

Mennonites in Mexico are farmers. Very few of the 12,000 Mennonites earn their living any other way. Those who do are the exceptions that prove the rule. The farming methods among the Mennonites are identical in all settlements. Everywhere they farm in semi-arid regions and nowhere do they practice irrigation except on a small scale for garden and orchard purposes. The farming is of a diversified nature but is restricted because of climatic conditions.

The principal crop grown in recent years has been oats. It has been found that the sparse rainfall and short summer season render the production of good corn and wheat very difficult. The Mennonites found after experimentation that a hardy wheat imported from Canada produced a good crop the first year of planting, a negligible crop the second year, and did not mature at all the third.

Corn and beans, both of which grow well, are subject to vagaries of the weather. They are profitable crops without supplemental irrigation. At the present time the oats produced by the Mennonites is yielding what for them, after many years of difficult struggle, is a substantial return for their work. It has been estimated that the annual net profit totals about three hundred dollars per family.

By comparison with the Mexicans, the Mennonites are superior farmers. It is estimated that one-fifth of the Mennonites use tractors and modern power machinery. This way of farming is in sharp contrast with the native Mexican who may be operating a small ox-drawn hand plow which merely scrapes a few inches below the surface. Mennonites who have no tractors use horses. Nowhere does one see Mennonites use oxen or donkeys.

It is refreshing to visit Mennonite settlements in contrast to the brown barren Mexican villages because of the way the wide streets are lined with trees and many houses are half-secluded from view by clusters of trees around them. Shade and fruit trees are grown in all the villages. Although rotation of crops is not possible to a large degree, very many Mennonites have developed fine gardens and small orchards where a variety of common fruits and vegetables are grown.

It is truly remarkable to note how much industry, thrift, and modern methods of farming can do in a short span of years. What had once been an uninhabited and desolate stretch of semi-arid prairie land, over which nothing but long horned cattle roamed, has been transformed into a series of prosperous agricultural villages surrounded by fields of grain, green pastures, and herds of fine sleek cattle. The traveler through those parts of Mexico where Mennonites are settled is impressed with the fine large draft horses of the Mennonites in contrast to the small scrawny Mexican horses of the natives. Dairy cattle and hogs, too, are well fed and of much finer quality than the small, bony native stock.

BUSINESS AND INDUSTRY

The Old Colony Mennonites are definitely opposed to their members engaging in business and industry, and members are forbidden to live in towns. However, a number of small general stores and blacksmiths are to be found in the villages. The village of Neuhorst in the Durango Colony has an ice plant and cold storage lockers. The two men who operate this business are both farming on the side. In the village of Rosenthal in the Manitoba Colony there is a small establishment in which a combination stationery store, drug store, and print shop are operated. The operator is a self-educated dentist who, besides pulling teeth and making plates, also serves as a bone-setter. In times of emergency he also serves as a practical doctor. It is interesting to note that in this little print shop with the help of three or four adolescents, a German song book, a catechism, and the New Testament in German have been printed, the type being set by hand by the four youthful employees.

The largest and most promising Mennonite business in Mexico is that operated by a General Conference Mennonite family in the city of Cuauhtemoc. This city serves as the main trading center for the 10,000 Mennonite settlers in Chihuahua. This family came to Cuauhtemoc as a penniless refugee family in the late twenties, the father buying merchandise in the larger cities and peddling it with horse and wagon through the Old Colony villages. Today the father and his three sons are the largest merchandisers and manufacturers in Cuauhtemoc as well as the only large Mennonite business establishment in Mexico. They operate a large general store and farm implement business in Cuauhtemoc, a large cheese factory on the edge of town, plus a number of small cheese factories in the villages, a large wholesale and retail grain buying and selling business, and at the present time are erecting a slaughter house and an ice plant on the outskirts of Cuauhtemoc. These Mennonites derive the largest share of their business from the Old Colony people and in turn provide a market for the goods produced on their farms. Because of their industriousness and business insight they are doing much to develop the commercial and industrial phases of this area. A reputation has been gained throughout all Mexico for Mennonite cheese, known as "Queso Imperial," manufactured by them. In the State of Durango, on a much smaller scale, a local farmer has developed a ready market for butter which he sells at the railroad station to traveling passengers. The butter, known as "Mantequilla Mennonita," is widely sought after by Mexican customers.

As long as the Old Colony Mennonites prohibit their members from entering business and industry, it is obvious that Mennonites in that country will never become industrial leaders. As is already evident, they provide opportunity for the few non-Old Colony Mennonites or Mexicans to develop these fields.

VI

How are the Mennonites Governed?

The Mennonites in Mexico are organized along lines very similar to Mennonite political organization in Russia. Each village has a Schulz or a mayor with wide executive powers who is elected every two years and cannot serve two terms in succession. All of the villages together elect an Oberschulz who is equivalent to a governor for the colony. Each colony has its own Oberschulz. The Oberschulz can be reelected as often as the electorate decides he has served satisfactorily. Only property owners and heads of families may vote. The village Schulzes and their assistants or secretaries meet once a year to discuss matters of general interest to the whole colony. These men are the elected administrative agents of their villages and are concerned with most contacts that need to be made with the outside world for either the villages or the colony. This pattern of organization is identical with that of the Old Colony and Sommerfelder Mennonites in Canada and Paraguay at the present time.

TAXES

The centralization of land ownership in the hands of one or two officials makes it very convenient for government officials to levy and collect taxes. The Oberschulz finds out from the local municipality what the total assessment for the year is, and then figures out the per acre cost and assesses each land owner accordingly. In addition to the property taxes, members are assessed for colony expenses, such as road repairing and financial remuneration allowed to the Oberschulz and his assistant for their work.

The only taxes levied by the Mexican Government are taxes on land, wagons, and animals sold or killed for home use. The Mexican Government trusts the Oberschulz to keep an accurate record of these items and to report once a year to pay the assessments. The taxes generally are very low. During 1943, for instance, the average tax per family amounted to about five dollars in American money.

LAW AND ORDER

At the present time none of the Old Colony Mennonites hold citizenship in Mexico. All of them have retained their Canadian citizenship, and according to present indications it appears that the young people coming of age will declare themselves Canadian rather than Mexican citizens. The Mennonites rely for protection upon the local government, something which was guaranteed them in their charter of special privileges. In the Durango colony repeated robberies and attacks on the Mennonites resulted in the stationing of a corps of twelve armed soldiers in one of the villages of the colony. The Mennonites built the barracks to house this police force. In the summer of 1944 the Government asked them also to share half the expense of maintaining this police force. After some discussions among themselves the Mennonites agreed to do this.

In twenty-one years of Mennonite residence in Mexico four Mennonites have been murdered and an unrecorded number of robberies and other violations committed. A considerable number of Mexican robbers have been killed in the Mennonite colonies by the armed guards while defending Mennonites. This raises an interesting question of consistency if the doctrine of non-resistance must be maintained by means of force and violence. It should be remembered, of course, that the case referred to above applies only to one small colony representing one-sixth of the total Mennonite population in Mexico.

VII
What is the Nature of the Old Colony Church?

The Church is at the very center of life in the Old Colonies, not on the periphery. Citizenship in the community means eventual membership in the Church, even if church membership is only nominal. Not to be a member is to choose ostracism and loss of social status. Obviously few men make this choice. Religious practices prevailing among the Old Colony Mennonites differ very little from practices in Russia a century ago. Worship is conducted in plain meeting houses which are equipped only with backless benches and little else.

CHURCH ORGANIZATION

The Church is efficiently organized. Each of the Old Colonies has one bishop and as many preachers as are needed for the various churches. In the largest colony, that of Manitoba with 7,200 souls, there are eleven preachers; in Durango, with 2,100 souls, there are six. There are several preachers in each congregation but neither preachers nor bishops receive financial remuneration for their services. Ministers are chosen from the lay members whenever needed but they receive no special training. Each colony also has one deacon whose duties are chiefly that of keeping the church record book and administering aid to the poor wherever it is needed. The final word of authority in matters pertaining to life and conduct in the colony rests with the preachers. Discipline is exercised on recalcitrant members by means of the ban or ex-communication. The threat of this form of punishment is often as effective as the punishment itself.

RELIGIOUS CUSTOMS

As far as this writer was able to discover, daily family worship, apart from silent grace before meals, was not practiced or even encouraged. Critical thinking about religious matters and church activities is discouraged. The church services are all conducted in the German language. The sermon is read in High German and expository comments are made in the Low German dialect, known as Platt-deutsch. The latter is partially necessary because many of the young people do not understand the High German. The dialect is the only language commonly spoken in the colonies. Schoolhouses are often used for worship services. In the smaller villages where there are no church houses conveniently located, the residents must drive to neighboring villages to attend church. The weekly Sunday worship service lasts from two to three hours. Special church services are held on all of the following religious holidays: Christmas, New Year, Epiphany, Easter, Ascension Day, and Pentecost. A special Thanksgiving Day is observed, usually the fifth Sunday before Christmas. Catechetical instruction is given from Easter to seven weeks following Easter. Baptism is administered usually to young men and women in their early twenties just prior to marriage. There are no Sunday Schools among any of the Mennonites in Mexico except in the General Conference congregation in Cuauhtemoc.

MORALS AND ETHICS

One aspect of the strength and vigor of any group's religious and educational life is the level of the moral and ethical conduct of its people. Among the Mennonites in Mexico there is the usual variety of opinions on this controversial subject. A number of the colony leaders feel that the moral and ethical conditions in the colony are constantly getting worse while others maintain that these conditions are about the same as they always have been. However, the observation of the writer, plus discussions with several of the more alert colony leaders, would lead to the conclusion that these conditions are not improving and, in fact, may be retrogressing. Even in this isolated and carefully regulated island of Mennonitism, one of the most highly respected preachers lamented the fact that a Mennonite's word was no longer the equivalent of his bond. He tended to blame it on the contact with the neighboring Mexicans and their loose ethical and moral standards. He felt that Mennonites were steadily becoming more lax ethically and morally. It is estimated that cigarette smoking is an accepted practice on the part of at least seventy-five percent of the men; drinking, too, is quite common, although not necessarily drunkenness. The American Vice-Consul at Chihuahua commented on the impropriety of conduct on the part of some Mennonites who came to that City. He felt that the high moral reputation Mennonites enjoyed earlier was beginning to decline.

The visit of this writer was entirely too brief to make any careful observation on so controversial a subject, but superficial external observations indicated evidences of spiritual dormancy, moral laxity and intellectual atrophy. There seems to be little that challenges the best interests and abilities of the members toward creative life and thought. If there is any consolation in this fact, one could say that moral conditions among the Mennonites are indeed considerably better than moral conditions among the neighboring Mexicans.

DISCIPLINE

Most of the disciplinary problems in the colony relate to young people who have not yet joined church. Ministers frequently complain that the misbehavior of the young people is regrettable but since they were not yet church members nothing can be done about such conduct. It seems that as soon as these young people join church and marry they tend to conform to the rules of the church and in this way also to the standards of conduct demanded by the group. Refusal to do so, of course, means ex-communication, an exceedingly severe penalty in an area where Mennonites are an island of religious brotherhood in a sea of secular and alien culture. It is significant in this connection to note the small number of Old Colony Mennonites who leave the colony. Several of the leaders of the Manitoba Colony recalled that in the course of twenty years only three young men had left the colony, and these young men had not joined church at the time they left. These men moved to town and secured employment there.

EDUCATION

A very definite concern of the Old Colony Church is education. It is the threat of losing control over education that caused them to come to Mexico. The statement "As the school so the Church," which one frequently hears repeated in the colony, is an indication both of the inter-relationship of Church and school, and of the importance with which they look upon controlling education.

Each village has its own school. The teacher is selected from one of the apt or interested male church members. Selected teachers receive no special training for their job.

Each village pays its own teacher. There is no centralized school system, no superintendent of schools or director of the educational program, and no uniform salary system, although allowances do not vary a great deal from colony to colony. The average monthly allowance is one hundred pesos, or about twenty American dollars. The money for the schools and the teachers' allowance is raised in two ways: One-half of the cost is derived from an assessment on land holdings according to the size of the holding; the other half is raised by assessing the parents of the children who attend school. Thus, a man with a large family of children must pay proportionately much more than the man with few or no children. The school term is usually from five to seven months in a year, running from November or December until about May. The boys attend school from the ages of seven to fourteen and the girls from seven to thirteen. Subjects taught are reading, writing, arithmetic, singing, Bible study, and catechism. The catechism taught in weekday school is of an introductory nature. Young people get further catechetical instruction from the ministers when they become candidates for baptism.

CRITICISMS OF EDUCATION

There are some discerning members of the Old Colony communities who are dissatisfied with the condition of the schools. They expressed to the writer a regret that both the schools and the teachers were of such inferior quality. Some felt that additional courses, such as history, geography, and nature study might be taught. The teaching is practically all done by rote and students are expected to memorize a given body of traditional knowledge. There seems to be no stimulation toward any type of critical or creative thinking.

An evidence of the low standard of education is the absence of reading material in the homes. The writer seldom found books or magazines in the homes. Only in a few cases were newspapers discovered, and these were German periodicals printed in the United States or Canada, the *Steinbach Post* being the most popular because it contained items of news about the Canadian homeland from which these Mennonites came.

VIII

What are some Distinctive Cultural Conditions and Social Customs?

The culture of the Old Colony Mennonites is a strange blending of religious brotherhood and modern individualism. In the colony there is individual ownership of private property with no restriction on the amount of material possessions one may acquire. On the other hand, there is great concern for the common welfare. Certain auxiliary organizations exist to give expression to this common concern. These auxiliary organizations are not strictly within the church. Nevertheless, they work toward the same end as the church. They are the instruments providing practical expression to the implications of religion.

WAISENAMT

There are two organizations in the Mennonite colonies which illustrate the mutual concern for recurring problems that arise in the colonies. The first of these is the *Waisenamt*. The *Waisenamt* was once a very familiar organization in all Mennonite communities with a Russian tradition. Brought from Russia to Canada and from Canada to Mexico, it is a kind of trust company to which delegates are elected to serve as *Waisenmanner*. The chief duties of the *Waisenmanner* are to look after the estates of orphans, widows, and old people who no longer can or want to look after their own business matters. These men are elected for a three-year term. When a parent or parents die, leaving minors, the *Waisenmanner* call a meeting of the interested members of the family and take charge of disposing of personal property and seeing that the estate is properly handled and distributed.

If the children are all minors, the *Waisenmanner* are responsible for investing the money. In the case of a mother's death, the husband must make a list of all the property and of its value and give this list to the *Waisenamt*. In case the husband is married again he must pay half the value of his goods to the *Waisenamt* who in turn distributes it to the children when they come of age. If the husband does not remarry he is not compelled to pay anything to the *Waisenamt*, unless the *Waisenmanner* should decide that he is spending his money unwisely and not concerning himself with the highest welfare of his children.

The *Waisenmanner* have great authority in seeing that estates are equitably distributed and fairly managed. They are not paid for their work. Their service is something of a guarantee that impartial but respected outside parties will deal objectively with minors, widows, and others who are in need of careful supervision and mature business counsel. It is obvious that such an organization plays an important part in the life of a community and can often prevent disputes and unfair treatment among selfish and jealous heirs.

BRANDSCHADENVERSICHERUNG

The second of these organizations is the Brandschadenversicherung. The Old Colony Mennonites in Manitoba, Swift Current, and the Hague Colony have an organization which provides systematic protection for losses from fire. There is one elected individual, known as the *Brandvorsteher*, or general director, in each colony, and each village has its *Brandschulz*, or local agent. None of these officers are paid for their services. It is considered an honor to be elected to one of these offices and one's service is held to be a contribution to the common good. The duty of each village agent is to get a list of the property of the head of each family and the value thereof. Twice a year he makes a report to the colony *Brandvorsteher*. Any changes that take place in the value of property holdings are reported. When there is a loss the local village agent notifies the colony agent, the loss is estimated, and the damages paid for. Losses very from year to year and from colony to colony, but the assessments are the same in all the colonies. Losses from fire throughout the colonies are comparatively low.

CUSTOMS

Culturally the Mennonites in Mexico lag somewhat behind Mennonites in most other areas. This is true even when compared with the Old Order Amish in the United States. While such Mennonite groups as the Amish still adhere to a very simple standard of living, they have, by contrast with the Mennonites in Mexico, acquired much greater material possessions. Amish people have resisted social change but they have taken on many more of the cultural traits of the world around them than have the Mennonites in Mexico. This is accounted for in part by the Spanish culture of the Mexicans in comparison with the German or English culture in areas surrounding the Amish. Participation in civil and political life is strictly forbidden. Any participation in such matters, even on a religious and social basis with other Mennonite groups, would be regarded as being unequally yoked with the world and hence strictly forbidden.

An interesting contrast between Mennonites and Mexicans is their attitude toward family life. The Mennonite farmer comes to town on his wagon with his wife and his children. He makes the weekly or monthly shopping trips a social affair for the entire family. The Mexican farmer on the other hand comes to town on horseback, leaving his wife and children at home. He is seldom seen with his wife in public. In town he spends considerable time in bar rooms or on the street corner idly wasting time. The Mennonite families also tend to be larger in size. Families of twelve and fifteen are not uncommon, and the average Mennonite family in Mexico consists of six members.

Compared with Mennonites in other parts of the world the level of living in Mexico is low. The food is exceedingly simple with very little variety. Few homes have running water and none of them have such modern conveniences as bathrooms or electrical appliances. Women still have the status of peasant women throughout the world; they do much of the work around the barn, such as taking care of the dairy, the poultry, the gardens, and help their husbands in the fields. Women do not participate in public life and have no voice in church or community affairs.

In dress the lay people as well as the preachers conform to long established conventionalities. White collars, ties, bearded chins, and such vanities as watch chains and rings are strictly forbidden. Women likewise are garbed in conventional apron-dresses of somber colored cloth, plain cut after uniform and prescribed patterns. All women at all times wear shawls as head coverings. Both black and white shawls are worn; most of them are homemade. Many of the women and men go barefooted. Little girls dress in patterns identical with those of their mothers, and little boys follow the fashion of their fathers. Preachers, too, have a conventional dress, which consists of black shirts and old-fashioned sailor trousers tucked in high-topped black polished boots. The dress of the preachers differs from the lay people only on Sunday.

The houses are almost without exception of adobe brick; only a few are made of wood. Usually they are one story high and consist of four or five rooms at the most. Many of the young couples start married life in a single one-room house, this one room serving as dining room, bedroom, and living room for the family. Practically all of the Mennonite homes in Mexico have an outside kitchen in which the cooking is done. This is to avoid heating the house and attracting flies. The furnishings are exceedingly simple, most of the furniture having been brought along from Canada or made locally. Mennonites are generally self-sufficient, buying very little in stores except those things which they cannot produce themselves.

HEALTH AND HYGIENE

The latest hygienic methods and sanitary devices are unknown to the Mennonites of Mexico. Many of the homes have only sand or clay floors. In the better homes the floors are of wood or of tile; walls sometimes are plastered inside and stuccoed on the outside. It was a source of great surprise to the writer to observe the common practice of spitting on the floor, even in the better homes of the colony. Seeing this in connection with the children playing around on the floors shocks the sensibilities of a hygiene-conscious American.

The mortality rate for the Mennonites due to various diseases is unknown, but it is obviously much higher than in an area where hygienic conditions are better and health protection more widely accepted. There are no Mennonite doctors in any of the Mennonite colonies. When doctors are needed Mennonites go to the larger cities for medical advice and assistance from Mexican doctors. As is customary with many isolated and culturally retarded groups, the concept of preventive medicine is unknown. Doctors are resorted to only when patients are extremely sick and when diseases have made advances to the point where symptoms are externally observable. Since the colonies are removed from the cities anywhere from ten to seventy miles and since Mennonites have no automobiles or telephones, it is obvious that medical protection is very inadequate. A community hospital is at the present time being completed in the City of Cuauhtemoc, but outside of the Mennonites in that city there is very meager support from the Mennonites in the colonies for this project.

ATTITUDE TOWARD AUTOMOBILES

Modern devices are generally proscribed. This includes the automobile but not the use of the modern tractor for farming. About twenty percent of the Mennonite farmers own tractors and operate modern power equipment. Of interest to the writer was the fact that automobiles as automobiles were prohibited, but that all the parts of automobiles are regularly used. Motor cars are frequently purchased and immediately dissected. The motors of the demounted cars are used for farm purposes, such as water pumps or gasoline engines for belt power. The most common vehicle for transportation is an improvised wagon consisting of an automobile chassis to which is attached a wagon tongue and on which is placed a wagon body. The complete automobile seats and backs are removed from the cars and placed on the wagon body. The rubber-tire wheels and the spring cushions in the seats assure comfortable riding even if horse drawn. This provides a unique vehicle of transportation which can only properly be designated as an auto-wagon.

The curiosity of the writer was aroused as to why all the parts of the automobile could be used but not the unified whole. Upon inquiry from one of the elderly preachers it was discovered that the opposition to the use of the car was frankly a device for social control. The preacher claimed that it was easier to keep the young people of the colony together when only horse and wagon were permitted. No strong opposition to trucks was held, but it was felt that if trucks were allowed it would become difficult to draw the line between trucks for business purposes and trucks that might be used as pleasure vehicles.

IX

What do Mexicans and Mennonites think of Each Other?

THE ATTITUDE OF MEXICANS TOWARD THE MENNONITES

The Federal and state governments of Mexico are exceedingly friendly toward the Mennonites at the present time. Avila Camacho, the present President of Mexico, has on several occasions told Mennonite delegations visiting him that Mexico desires a Mennonite settlement in every one of the twenty-eight Mexican states. He said that they provided the best possible demonstration farms for the Mexicans and at no cost to the government. The various governors of the states seem to be competing with each other to attract Mennonite settlers to their respective states. They outdo each other in offering attractive terms and promising assistance to Mennonites who are willing to settle in their states because of the contribution they expect the Mennonites to make to agricultural development.

The Mennonites are looked up to by the Mexicans as model farmers. In the State of Durango the writer was told of a government experimental farm that had been in operation not far from the Mennonite Colony. This farm was said to have been recently abandoned because the government claimed that Mennonite farms and farming methods could be observed without cost and that the students could learn more about farming in this manner than they could in their own experimental station. Whatever the facts in the case, the experimental farm is no longer in operation and the Mexicans spend much time observing the Mennonite farmers. The common people seem to show a neutral attitude of curiosity rather than one of hostility or friendliness.

Some of the more thoughtful Mexicans are more critical in their attitude toward the Mennonites. They consider them a peaceful, hardworking people with some knowledge of agriculture and the ability to develop areas, but they also look with suspicion upon them because the Mennonites remain isolated from their Mexican neighbors and, as far as possible, resist all aspects of Mexican culture. They make no effort to teach Mexicans better methods of agriculture, they refuse to learn the native language except when it is necessary for business transactions with the natives, they forbid intermarriage and frown upon social contacts with the Mexicans generally. One Mexican school teacher told the writer that the Mennonites in Mexico lack a sense of beauty and an appreciation of art.

Mennonites are admired for their fair dealings with Mexicans, for their peaceful attitudes, and for their quiet way of settling disputes, but their cultural isolation and their implied superiority raise the question of future relations with the native Mexicans. Some Mexicans look with disfavor upon Mennonites who come to Mexico in large numbers and refuse to identify themselves with the country. A rural sociologist attached to the United States Embassy in Mexico City, and very familiar with rural conditions throughout the whole of Mexico, said that the more thoughtful Mexicans are deeply concerned with what he considered an inevitable fundamental conflict between Mennonites and Mexicans. He said Mexicans speak flatteringly on the one hand and skeptically on the other about Mennonite settlers. On the whole, however, Mennonites have nothing to fear at present, neither from an unfriendly attitude on the part of the people nor on the part of the official governments.

ATTITUDES OF THE MENNONITES TOWARD MEXICANS

The attitude of the Mennonites toward Mexico is one of general satisfaction with their religious freedom and their economic status. They enjoy the complete absence of government regulation on matters pertaining to religion, education, and agriculture. They unanimously agree that the central government has been fair, considerate, and loyal to its promises to the Mennonites. Whenever delegations have been sent to the central government to discuss issues relative to their welfare they have been cordially received and their petitions in every case have been granted. Only in 1935 was there a vigorous conflict when the federal government attempted to introduce public school education into the Mennonite colonies. This was successfully resisted, but success came only after a long, hard struggle and upon threat of leaving Mexico if complete freedom of education, as originally granted in 1921, would be denied.

While there has been general satisfaction with state and Federal governments, there is a feeling that local government is unstable and very often openly corrupt. The bribery and graft which seems to be an accepted custom among public officials and among business men is very distasteful to the Mennonites. Because of the instability of the local governments and the unscrupulousness of some of the natives, Mennonites have suffered severely through exploitation, robberies, and in several cases even murder. During these trying years some of the Mennonites temporarily forgot their non-resistant principles and threatened attacking bandits with weapons. This was not generally approved but members who used weapons were not disciplined by the church for it.

One unmistakable evidence of the Mennonites' attitude toward Mexico is their unwillingness to become Mexican citizens. 1944 marks the twenty-first year of residence of the Mennonites in Mexico. Children born during the first year of residence are, therefore, called upon to declare their citizenship. Upon inquiry as to which country they would claim, it was found that the majority would claim Canada. This is somewhat strange in view of their flight from Canada because of the denial of freedom and the generous privileges they have enjoyed in Mexico. Perhaps it is explained in part by the remark of one of the influential leaders among the Mennonites in Mexico who said that he had always felt that Mennonite settlement in Mexico was temporary and that it was preliminary to settlement somewhere else. For some unexplainable reason he said he felt that God would open new doors for Mennonites in another area.

Although there is general optimism with regard to the future economic outlook in Mexico, there is considerable evidence that the Mennonites are not yet deeply rooted in that country. The writer was told that Mennonites in Mexico did not hesitate to recommend the country to other Mennonites wishing to settle there if the reasons for their coming were sufficiently strong to enable them to endure the disappointments and hardships which could certainly be expected. He was told that nobody should think of settling in Mexico if he came only because of a desire to find bright economic opportunities. Mennonites should not go to Mexico unless they are prepared to settle in groups of twenty-five to fifty families.

The situation in Mexico is very similar to the situation among the Mennonites in Russia a generation ago. Mennonites are a rural cultural group. They are looked up to by the Mexicans as a culturally superior group. The Mennonites on the other hand tend to look condescendingly upon the native Mexicans, just as did the Mennonites in Russia upon the native peasants. The Mexicans are hired to do menial tasks at low wages, but little effort is made to understand the problems and the culture of the Mexican people. There is, of course, no social intercourse except that which is necessary through business transactions and labor relations. This attitude does not promise good future relations.

X

What is the Future of Mennonites in Mexico?

The question naturally arises as to the future of Mennonites in Mexico. There is also a general interest in knowing whether Mexico is a land which holds promise for further agricultural colonization. We shall list first the factors in favor of colonization as they would appeal to a non-resistant agricultural religious group, such as the Mennonites.

In the first place, Mexico guarantees religious freedom and has a record of twenty-one years in which to show that it has fulfilled its promises. Those fleeing from country to country for the sake of religious freedom will appreciate this fact above every other.

Second, there is a friendly attitude on the part of the state and national governments toward agricultural colonists who can improve the land and develop agricultural resources. Mexico is at present eager to develop its country along all lines and for this reason warmly welcomes agricultural groups.

Third, land is inexpensive and the agricultural level is very low, thus providing an opportunity for skilled groups to demonstrate better ways of farming. In other words, a certain type of agricultural missionary opportunity now exists in Mexico.

Fourth, Mexico provides a place in which to live simply, inexpensively, and isolated from urbanized and industrialized societies. Because of the warmer climate the problem of housing and shelter is not so expensive as in the cooler climatic regions.

Fifth, Mexico offers limited opportunity for those who wish to pioneer in a foreign country that needs to be agriculturally and industrially developed.

Sixth, Mexico has large areas of arid and semi-arid lands which could be brought under cultivation by means of irrigation projects.

Factors Unfavorable for Colonization

Over against the factors which favor Mexico as a place for future colonization are a list of counter factors which make Mexico an undesirable place for religious group settlement.

First, Mexico as a country has a Latin culture which includes the Spanish language, the Roman Catholic religion, lower moral standards, and a heritage and customs alien to that of the Mennonites who are a Protestant, Germanic religious group with generally high ethical and moral standards.

Second, Mexican local and national governments are more unstable, and democracy more immature, than is the case in local and national governments in the United States and Canada. Mexico is a democracy in name only, not in fact. The common people actually have nothing to say about the government under which they live.

Third, while Mexico has plentiful land, most of it needs to be irrigated to be made productive. This requires huge amounts of capital. In many areas the rainfall is insufficient to supply enough water for irrigation even if it is dammed up and stored for that purpose. The sub-surface water supply is inadequate in many places so that it cannot be pumped to irrigate the arid regions which abound in Mexico.

Fourth, natural rainfall in many areas is strictly limited to rainy seasons. This means that only certain crops can be grown during these seasons because of the short growing period. For people who have been used to areas of abundant rainfall and a long growing season, this factor would make it a very difficult location in which to farm with enthusiasm.

Fifth, freedom of religion as enjoyed by the Mennonites is only a special privilege granted on the basis of a presidential decree. It is not a congressional provision for all minority groups. It can be revoked at any time without advance notice. This raises the question of the permanency of the privileges and also whether Mennonites as a Christian body want to accept a privileged status.

Sixth, Mexico as a country is responding to various pressures brought by the United States Government to conform to such matters as universal military training and peace time conscription. Mexico has adopted many political and economic measures similar to those adopted in the United States.

It is not the purpose of the writer to decide for individuals or groups whether Mennonites should or should not colonize in Mexico. However, he would agree with the sage opinion of one of the Old Colony leaders in Mexico, that no migration to Mexico should take place unless the individuals concerned have as their reason for going the search for religious freedom. From the purely economic standpoint, there are many areas in the United States, Canada, or Alaska that offer as great or greater possibilities than Mexico.

CONCLUSION

The future of the Mennonites in Mexico will be dependent upon several factors. Chief of these is the factor of political stability. The Old Colony Mennonites will probably continue to multiply and expand at their present rate, unless disturbed by change in political conditions which will threaten the privileges enjoyed at the present time. The same can be said for the Sommerfelder Mennonites. As for the three other Mennonite groups now in Mexico, unless they are strengthened numerically by sources from outside their own body—it is very likely that they will die out in the course of several generations or will be absorbed into the larger populations of Mexico. Cultural isolation among the Old Colony Mennonites will perhaps continue for generations to come, but each succeeding generation will find it more difficult to maintain its isolation than the previous one.

As to future colonization in Mexico by other Mennonite groups from Canada and the United States, this, too, depends primarily upon political developments in these countries. If permanent conscription becomes the accepted political policy in the United States and Canada, it may result in the migration of considerable numbers of Mennonites to Mexico. Such groups may prefer the economic privations and the cultural limitations accompanying religious freedom rather than material prosperity, coupled with the loss of religious freedom in the United States and Canada.

If political conditions continue much as they have in the past decades so that Mennonites in both countries will not feel that their freedom of religion is encroached upon, there remains a possibility of developing some inter-communication between the Old Colony Mennonites in Mexico and those in the United States and Canada. The writer found an interest on the part of Mennonites in both countries in each other. Valuable lessons by way of Christian community organization may be learned from the Mennonites of Mexico by the Mennonites of the United States and Canada. On the other hand, there are useful services which the Mennonites in these countries can render to their brethren in Mexico. It remains for the channels of intercommunication to be developed and contacts to be made. At any rate, Mennonites in North America should no longer continue to be ignorant of the life and needs of the large block of 12,000 of their brethren in Mexico.

I. POPULATION AND VILLAGES OF MENNONITES IN MEXICO ACCORDING TO BRANCH OF MENNONITES AND GEOGRAPHIC DISTRIBUTION

Old Colony Mennonites

1. Chihuahua — (a) Manitoba Colony — 7,225 Souls

   Villages —

Bergthal	Gnadenfeld	Neuendorf	Rosenheim
Blumenfeld	Gnadenthal	Neuenlage	Rosenort
Blumengart	Gruenthal	Neuhorst	Rosenthal
Blumenort	Hamburg	Neureinland	Schanzenfeld
Blumenstein	Hochfeld	Osterwick	Schoenthal
Blumenthal	Hochstaedt	Reinfeld	Schoenwiese
Chortitz	Hoffnungsfeld	Reinland	Silberfeld
Eichenfeld	Kleefeld	Reinthal	Steinbach
Einlage	Kronsgart	Rosenbach	Thalbach
Friedensruh	Kronsthal	Rosenfeld	Waldheim
	Neuenburg	Rosengart	Weidenfeld

2. (b) Swift Current Colony — 2,122 Souls

   Villages —

Burwalde	Grossweide	Neuhoffnung	Rosenhof
Blumenheim	Gruenfeld	Neuricht	Schoenberg
Blumenhof	Neuenlage	Neustaedt	Schoendorf
No. 108 (No Name)	No. 114 (No Name)		Schoenfeld

3. Durango — Hague Colony — 2,151 Souls

   Villages —

Blumenhof	Hochfeld	Neuhorst	Rosenfeld
Blumenort	Hochstadt	Neustadt	Rosenort
Gruenfeld	Neuanlage	Reinfeld	Schoenfeld
Gruenthal	Neuhoffnung	Reinland	Schoenthal

4. Nuevo Leon —New Manitoba Colony — 200 Souls

   Villages —

Chortitz	Neuhoffnung	Reinland	Rosengart

Sommerfelder Colony — Approximately 600 Souls

Chihuahua

   Villages —

Blumenthal	Neuanlage	Schoenthal	Sommerfeld
		Silberfeld	Weidefeld

Church of God in Christ, Mennonite — 65 Souls

Chihuahua — Camp No. 45

General Conference — 50 Souls

Chihuahua — Hoffnungsau Congregation in Cuauhtemoc

Coahuila — One Family — 5 Souls

Old Order Mennonite and Old Order Amish — 36 Souls

San Luis Potosi — Six families

11. POPULATION GROWTH IN DURANGO COLONY

(Prepared June 28, 1944, by Johann P. Wall)
(From the Annual Church Census Records
Taken Each December 15th)

Year	Births	Deaths	No. of Members	Total Souls	Annual Net Increase
1925	—	—	182	477	—
1926	24	13	293	770	393
1927	19	30	325	892	118
1928	—	—	—	—	—
1929	42	18	350	980	88
1930	48	13	379	1049	69
1931	55	20	406	1130	81
1932	63	14	417	1169	39
1933	58	15	430	1212	43
1934	64	9	512	1397	85
1935	44	18	553	1440	43
1936	100	29	580	1511	71
1937	70	20	574	1550	39
1938	97	24	676	1637	87
1939	95	21	675	1774	127
1940	—	—	—	—	—
1941	92	22	767	1972	198
1942	107	40	791	2027	55
1943	115	16	856	2151	124

There are at present 401 families in the **Durango Colony.**
Immigration from Canada continued 1925-1927.

Records for 1928 and 1940 unavailable.

III. DURANGO OLD COLONY MENNONITE LAND

HOLDINGS
According to Plowable Land and Pasture
For Each Village

Village	Plowable Land Acres	Plowable Land Acres	Total
Gruenfeld	1980.94	1158.43	3139.37
Blumenort	1558.57	1467.18	3025.75
Neuanlage	824.98	1561.04	2386.02
Reinland	1052.22	1906.84	2959.06
Rosenfeld	311.22	1635.14	1946.36
Neuhoffnung	227.24	2035.28	2262.52
Hochfeld	521.17	755.82	1276.99
Gruenthal	2677.48	1227.59	3905.07
Schoenfeld	1630.20	1067.04	2697.24
Neustaedt	797.81	486.59	1284.40
Hochstaedt	1854.97	1200.42	3055.39
Reinfeld	528.58	652.08	1180.66
Neuhorst	2134.08	696.54	2830.62
Blumenhof	1499.29	733.59	2232.88
Rosenort	1353.56	3156.66	4510.22
Schoenthal	2215.59	738.53	2954.12
Total	21,167.90	20,478.77	41,646.67